Ancient Magick for Today's Witch Series

WICCAN SPELLS

MONIQUE JOINER SIEDLAK

OSHUN
PUBLICATIONS
oshunpublications.com

Wiccan Spells © Copyright 2016 by Monique Joiner Siedlak

ISBN ISBN: 978-1-948834-08-7 (Paperback)

ISBN 978-1-948834-13-1 (eBook)

Cover Design by MJS

Cover Images by MidJourney

Published by Oshun Publications

www.oshunpublications.com

ANCIENT MAGICK FOR TODAY'S WITCH SERIES

The *Ancient Magick for Today's Witch Series* is a series for modern witches to explore ancient magick, covering Celtic, Gypsy, and Crystal magic, among others. It offers practical advice on spells, rituals, and enchantments for today's use, incorporating natural energies and spiritual connections. With insights into Shamanism, Wicca, and more, it helps readers enhance their magickal journey, offering paths to protection, prosperity, and spiritual growth by combining ancient wisdom with contemporary practice.

Wiccan Basics

Candle Magick

Wiccan Spells

Love Spells

Abundance Spells

Herb Magick

Moon Magick

Creating Your Own Spells

Gypsy Magic

Protection Magick

Celtic Magick

Shamanic Magick

Crystal Magic

Sacred Spaces

Solitary Witchcraft

Novice Witch's Guide

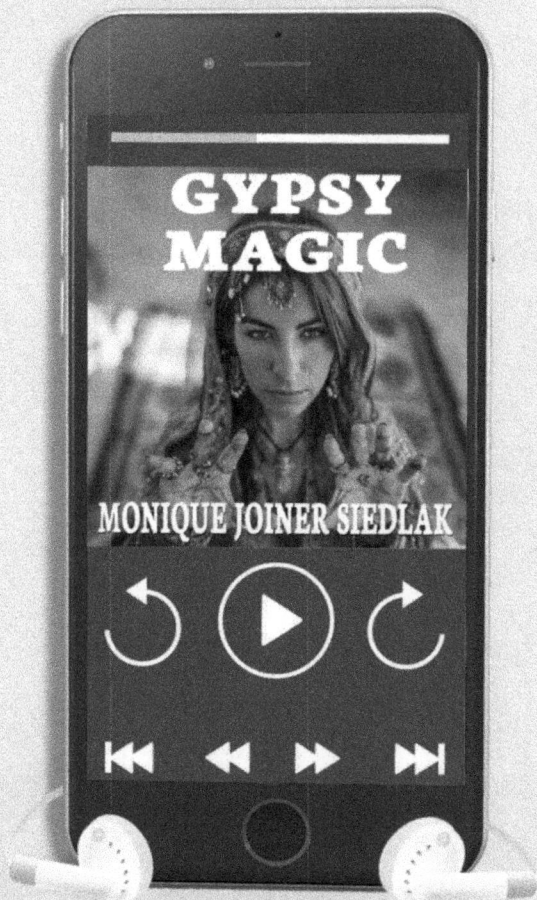

AVAILABLE IN AUDIO!

GYPSY MAGIC

MONIQUE JOINER SIEDLAK

mojosiedlak.com/audiobooks

CONTENTS

INTRODUCTION

Witchcraft refers to the practice and art of all things of the craft, such as spells, while the religion itself is known as Wicca. Though you can make a sharp distinction between the definitions of Witch and Wiccan, or Witchcraft and Wicca, most practitioners accept both words and identities. Wicca is a religion with many variations, it is a personally structured system, and one can only state generalities about its creed and form.

Wicca sees and knows that the Godhead is dual; it reveres God and Goddess. Both powerful and severe, warm and loving, all-present and all-knowing energy of and within the universe. Wicca goes on to tell us that our world, the physical world is one of a multitude of possible realities. The physical reality that we are made of and which we find ourselves a part of is not the highest form of existence, and of course, the spiritual, energetic world is in no way better or purer than the physical world. Wicca is a religion that utilizes magick, the most appealing and unique feature of this religion. Magick is the practice of moving natural energies to effect a needed change. Wicca and magick are often seen as interchangeable. However, Wicca is a religion that embraces magick. If one seeks only to practice magick, Wicca is not the answer for you.

At the core of Wicca, we find a joyful union with nature, and the Earth is a manifestation of divine energy. Meadows, forests, and beaches are the Wiccan's temples. When a Wiccan is outdoors, he or she is surrounded by the sacred sanctity of Earth. Wiccans listen to the Earth, and when a Wiccan loses touch with our beautiful planet, they lose touch with the deity. At its most basic, magick is the science of Earth's hidden powers, for a real Wiccan, there is nothing supernatural about magick. Wicca is a beautiful religion; it is a personal and positive celebration of life available to all who seek it. Perhaps we could say what you seek is seeking you. Whether you are new to Wicca or already a practitioner of the magickal arts, I'd like to welcome you to Wicca and spell casting. If you are reading this guidebook, you are already on your magickal path. I wish you all the best on your journey. Blessed be.

1

THINGS TO CONSIDER WHEN CASTING A SPELL

Magick spells come in many forms. What separate a magickal spell from any other action you make daily are you, your intent, goals, and desire. A magick spell is a conscious attempt to manipulate power and energy to achieve your personal goal. There are many types of spells, using many kinds of ingredients. Not all spell styles will suit the individual practitioner; therefore, it is essential to find the method that you are most comfortable with. There is only one component of every magick spell that cannot be replaced. You and the energy you give to the spell.

Experience and Knowledge

It's simple to understand that a novice will be less skilled at magick than an experienced one. While you study and practice, you'll develop the skills used in magick. You'll additionally learn what skills works best for you.

Working with energy is an art, and you achieve this by shifting your consciousness to reach that magickal place in your mind, spirit, and body. It is essential to know when to act and when not to act.

Effort and Intention

Spells are essentially created on desire, feeling, and will. While you could perform a spell precisely as it's written, with no blunders or errors, it still won't be successful if you don't drive your intention and energy into your effort. See, it's not just the words you say, the tools you use, or even the acts you perform that make magick work, it's what you put into the spell that's important. You can use visualization; raise your energy, meditation and other techniques to add that energy into your spells. Do everything you do in your spells purposefully and with intention. It's my opinion that, when using magick to make an effect happen, the most important thing is to want it intensely and to will it to happen.

For example, if you were to cast a spell out of anger, this action's consequences could have adverse effects. It would be best to understand how to build up a strong belief in yourself and your power and Wicca. You also need to recognize that you do not achieve your desired result in some cases, as it is not meant to be. As a witch, you must know who you are and be aware of your positive and negative traits. You have to know, understand, and ultimately improve yourself or, at least, your attitudes and behavior. A real witch is always willing to change. It takes maturity and self-awareness to know who you are in your deepest parts. There is no substitute for life experience, be it good or bad, the witch knows this and uses it in their magick.

Magick is potent and can be dangerous if misused. You must have respect for magick because it is governed by universal laws that can't be broken. A witch understands that life is one vast learning experience. Witches are forever expanding their knowledge by reading articles and books; a witch is always a student. Witches continuously practice their craft to strengthen their magickal abilities. After all, practice makes perfect. Having patience and becoming receptive to the results of the spells they cast is essential. Magick itself isn't black or white. The more effort you put into working towards a goal, the faster the universe will deliver on the desire that has been set.

Timing

The time of day, day of the week, moon phase, seasons, astrological position, and more, can all be symbolic and significant in spell casting. For example, if you were to do a spell to help you succeed in a new endeavor, you might like to cast it on the first day of the new moon, as this moon phase signifies new beginnings. Then the moon growing full can symbolize your success increasing. Do some investigation to see what different times and events mean and if you want to include their significance.

Symbolism

You'll find that magick depend greatly on symbolism. Everything used in spell craft symbolize something. As a result of being aware of what specific things mean and using them in agreement with your intentions, you can insert meaning and importance to everything you do, which can benefit your mentality and make your spells more successful. Be certain to use symbols that you find significant and that make sense to you.

Your Health and Well-Being

Spells have a habit of being less successful if you are physically, mentally, distressed, distracted, emotionally tired or else not in an ideal condition for spellwork,. Many individuals prefer to do some type of pre-ritual to get them in the correct state of mind. Overall, make sure that you eat well, get enough sleep, deal with stress efficiently, and keep yourself healthy.

2

GROUNDING AND CENTERING

Grounding and centering are an integral part of the spell work process and are indeed an essential part of many other aspects of Wicca. Grounding and centering allow the Wiccan to be calm, focused, clear-minded, and able to hold the spell's intention without being distracted or disturbed by intrusive thoughts. We can ground and center ourselves with simple deep breathing exercises and a short meditation, or we can use the methods detailed below.

A witch needs to ground and center themselves before performing any spell work as being grounded and centered helps to bring calm to our emotions. A witch will use the ground as a focal point for energy and establish a deeper level of connection with the Earth.

Grounding yourself before doing spell work is vital for the following reasons:

- It increases balance and stability to your emotional and physical state.
- It helps us to accept that we have a purpose.

- It brings us strength.
- It makes the release of energy easier.
- It allows us to attain higher spiritual levels when working with spells.

There are many techniques for grounding; a classic type of grounding is to imagine roots growing into the Earth from your bare feet and spinal column, like a tree taking root in the ground. It is an excellent idea to call the Earth to ask permission and thank her for her healing energy.

Centering is a way to self-awareness, owning your energy, and knowing yourself. To tune into the Earth's rhythms, a witch will use all his or her senses to establish a connection to the Earth. Centering is your groundwork for any magickal spell you wish to try. Connecting to the Earth helps to center you and your magick. As a starter, gather one of the following for each sense:

- For touch – Use a dish filled with soil.
- For taste – Dissolve a pinch of sea salt in a glass of warm mineral water.
- For sound – Choose a recording of nature sounds.
- For scent – Light incense.
- For sight – Use a picture of a beautiful place in nature that resonates with you.

Please choose a time and place where you can work undisturbed. When you are ready to begin, play your nature sounds, light a candle and your incense, place your dish of soil and picture in front of you, dip your finger in the warm salt water and place a drop of it on your tongue then begin a meditation session. When you feel relaxed, shift your attention to nature sounds, and slowly focus on your picture while maintaining awareness of your senses. Also, remember to keep your breathing regulated. Using this technique, you will feel centered and in touch with the Earth and your senses, a beautiful state to be in just before starting a spell. Being grounded and centered is the ideal way to be when casting a spell as you are aware of your senses and the Earth, which will make your spell more effective and powerful.

3

CASTING YOUR CIRCLE

Every person needs a place to work. Whether you are a baker in a kitchen, a surgeon in an operating theatre, or a mechanic in a workshop, you will need a safe, comfortable place to get the job done. It is no different for a Wiccan. To cast a spell, you will need a safe, quiet, physical space and a safe spiritual place in which to do your work. To create this space to do your magickal work, you will need to 'cast a circle.' In essence, casting a circle is to form a spiritual-energetic place with energetic walls to keep you safe and undisturbed, where you can focus your power while you cast spells.

Circle-casting is a foundation skill every witch should learn. Circle-casting is the practice of setting up a temporary space for magick. The magick circle can be seen as a mobile temple. A circle is a psychic boundary between a witch and what she is casting and any interference that she could encounter. Casting a circle is a way to shut out distractions and stay focused on your spell work. Many witches cast a circle with psychic protection in mind. A witch can cast a circle with or without tools such as the athame (ceremonial blade), a length of cord, stones, or candles.

One of the simplest tools needed for circle casting is salt; however, all circle casting methods call for concentration and belief that the circle is real. A traditional circle has four cardinal points linked to the four directions, the four elements, and the Wiccan seasonal calendar, which usually represent the season solstice i.e., the winter solstice. Each witch will find their natural flow for how they want to cast a circle. There are many varied approaches to do so, but here is an example of a straightforward way to cast a circle.

Make sure you have everything you need for your ritual before casting your circle. There's nothing more frustrating than to realize that you've forgotten something and leaving to go fetch them. If you need to leave for something in the middle of a ritual, you may find it helpful to visualize "cutting" out a door that you would seal up when you return. This way, your circle is not broken.

Visualize a ring of light at the edge of the ritual space; this light will purify the circle's area. Breathe deeply and focus on the energy within your own body. When you feel warm energy reaches the circle's boundary, clap your hands together and say, "The circle is cast." With that, your circle will be cast.

The circle should be large enough to contain the witch and his or her ritual items. Once you have performed your ritual or spell, the circle must be taken down by ringing a bell, visualizing the circle dissolving, or putting your ritual tools away. Dissolving a circle helps to displace the energies you have used within the circle. If you don't take down the circle, that's okay; it will dissolve within a few minutes or hours, Numerous factors will help dissolve the circle faster, such as movement by people or animals. Leaving a circle open usually doesn't affect anyone negatively but can be an attraction for something that doesn't belong there, such as an evil entity.

4

SPELL CASTING

Spells in magick is a broad topic, covering many different methods and means. For the Wiccan, the spell is a robust method of directing energy to achieve a particular result.

When we consider casting a spell, we often think of witches in pointed hats muttering incantations and pointing wands at people, changing boys into frogs. Other people may think of Harry Potter, making feathers float with the flick of the wrist. In reality, a spell can be something as simple as saying a prayer. A spell is the direction of energy to achieve a particular outcome, and the Wiccan will sometimes use additional items such as wands, crystals, talismans, or herbs to help strengthen the energy they are directing. Many regular people who aren't Wiccan cast spells every day; they just don't know it. Saying "bless you" when someone sneezes or "gesundheit" when someone burps can be considered spells as they all involve you wishing intent upon someone and directing energy to a specific end.

Casting a successful spell requires the correct mindset and circumstances, but it is not any of those things. We shouldn't focus on the superficial when we attempt to cast a spell. If we are too caught up in making sure that it is the exact right time with the right ingredients or burning the correct incense, then the point of our spell casting may be lost as it has become an exercise in fashion as opposed to results-driven spiritual action.

The one basic principle to follow above all is that paraphernalia is about focusing your consciousness. Or to present it in another way, to build up your belief. The following are needed to cast a spell:

- Intent
- Focus
- Ability to shift your consciousness
- Trust in the universal energy and the Goddess
- Know your desire is being dealt with
- Patience
- Willingness to action your spell towards your goal

It is always an excellent idea to journal on the subject before you cast a spell. Preparation and planning are crucial when considering what spells to cast. Here are some questions you should work through before casting a spell.

- What do you want from the spell?
- What is the driving force or desire behind the spell?
- Are you aware of whether or not you may be manipulating your target?
- Are you going to work towards your desired outcome once the spell is cast?
- Do you genuinely believe that you can summon and channel the necessary energy to ensure the spell is effective?

- Do you have faith in the machinations of the universe and its ability to grant your wish?
- Will you take full responsibility for the outcomes of your actions as the spell caster?
- Are you confident that you have the knowledge to cast the spell successfully?
- Is it the right time? Perhaps your spell would be more potent in a day or two when moon phases or tides are different.
- Is your spell for the highest good?

Considering all these factors before you cast a spell will help you determine how the spell will manifest. Being sure of the purpose and intent behind a spell enables you to be more in tune with yourself and the spell you have cast.

5

THE BOOK OF SHADOWS

Many people in many different religions, crafts, and professions refer to or keep a sort of manual or guidebook on their work. Doctors and medical professionals refer to the International Classification of Diseases, composed and updated regularly by other medical professionals. Vehicle appraisers use the Kelley Blue Book, written and updated regularly by vehicle experts to value vehicles. The Wiccan uses the Book of Shadows to write down, store and create spells, potions, and all other magical writings.

A Book of Shadows is a book consisting of religious texts, rituals, and spells from a Wiccan tradition, also referred to as a grimoire. Gerard Gardner founded Wicca in the 1940s and named the book, the Book of Shadows. Traditionally, each coven would have a single copy of the book, kept by the coven's high priestess. Modern witches today may practice as a solitary practitioner. Nevertheless, there are no rules fixed in stone about the Book of Shadows. Most witches carry their own book, and it is very personalized to the witch who owns it. Formerly the Book of Shadows would be burnt upon the death of the witch. However, today, witches may pass on their magick book to another witch or family member. The Book of Shadows can be seen as a journal of your magickal and ritual practices which you have already done or would like to try.

There is a wide variety of mediums a Witch can use for their Book of Shadows, the most frequently used ones are simple notebooks, binders, journals or scrapbooks. Modern witches may even have a digital Book of Shadows on their computers or cell phones. There is no specific way to manage your book in today's world. Whatever means is most convenient for the witch is the way they should keep it.

A practical and straightforward way to organize your book of shadows is to combine all the information gathered into one book. You can separate your book into sections or use a modern bullet journal system. This way, you keep all your notes in one place. A simple version will have page numbers, cover sheet, and an index. Most witches write a spell to protect their book on the first page. Numerous witches like to enhance their book of shadows, although this is an individual choice. When writing in your book of shadows, consider it a ritual that you follow each time, light some candles, your favorite incense, and form your casting circle. Write with intent and take care of your handwriting. Use your book to reflect on spells and rituals and their outcomes. Remember, your Book of Shadows does not need to be perfect; it is your magick book, and imperfections can add beauty to the Book of Shadows. The Book of Shadows is a wonderful source of information that will be part of your magickal journey for as long as you practice Wicca.

Why You Need a Book of Shadows

A witch needs a Book of Shadows to put down in words all the magickal things they have learned and discovered on their journey. It serves nearly as a journal for the witch to reflect on all that she has done, something for her to go back to. The following are examples of topics to be included in the Book of Shadows:

Spells

Write the spells you have created, spells you have learned, and spells you still want to try. Spells can come from various sources, such as your favorite Wiccan books or web pages.

Magick Theory

In this section, you can add rules, ethics, exercises, and techniques relating to spell work, divination, energy work, chakra work, meditation, or visualization techniques.

Sacred Text

Collect text that resonates with you as a Witch so that you can use them in your craft. You can also write your own. Examples can be poems, prayers, chants, song lyrics, and devotions.

Recipes

Kitchen witches love to write magickal recipes in their Book of Shadows. You can utilize your Book of Shadows to assemble recipes that will be practiced in your rituals and spells. Write down the magickal properties of the kitchen ingredients; write down recipes for incense, oils, brews, elixirs, and tinctures.

Herbs

Herbs are an excellent tool for witchcraft. Write down the magickal and medicinal properties of the herbs you use the most. If you can draw or sketch, you can draw pictures of the herbs you use. You can add herb drying techniques, gardening tips, and herbal tea recipes.

Crystals

Write a list of all your crystals and their corresponding healing properties in your Book of Shadows. It is also helpful to add techniques for cleansing and charging your crystals as well as crystal grid layouts.

The Wheel of the Year

Collect information relating to each pagan festival that you celebrate. A great idea is to have a section for each Sabbat, the folklore behind them, magickal correspondences for these Sabbats, rituals practiced on these festivals, crafts used, prayers used during the festival, and recipes made during the festival.

The Moon Cycles

Many witches use the moon cycles to enhance their magickal practice. Write down all you know about the moon in your Book of Shadows. Write the moon names during each part of the cycle, corresponding dates, the meaning of each moon cycle, and spells for each moon cycle.

Divination

Many witches practice this with tarot, your Book of Shadows is the right place to journal about your card readings and interpretation of the cards or create pages with the meanings of cards or tarot suites. In this section, you can add new tarot spreads you would like to try. Witches can also collect divination tools such as runes and pendulums.

Dreams

In your book of shadows, you can write down your dreams and understand their meanings. This is a powerful technique to enhance your psychic ability. This is best performed as soon as you can after the dream has taken place.

Astrology

Witches that enjoy astrology may have a section with star signs, moon signs, rising signs, ruling planets, corresponding colors, gemstones, and plants for each zodiac sign.

A final note on your Book of Shadows is to always listen to your intuition, do not hesitate to scrap something from your book and start anew; after all, it is your personal magickal book. Make the book your own, and don't be afraid to try new things and note them down; this adds to your knowledge and keeps track of your progress as you move along.

6

TYPES OF MAGIC

There are as many witchcraft paths as witches; always remember your magick is unique to you. The following types of magick are divided according to the source of energy rather than the way they do it. Please determine the one which is best for you, as it is your journey.

Natural Magick

Natural magick is a common form of magick, dealing with all the forces of nature, the ocean, the weather, crystals, and incorporating the four elements (Earth, Air, Water, and Fire). Natural magick is also known as folk magick and does not require a lot of preparation or tools. It can be practiced anywhere with what you have on hand. This type of magick has been practiced by shamans, healers, druids, and traditional witches for centuries. Examples of tools used for this type of magick include talismans, potions, and amulets.

Planetary Magick

Planetary magick draws its energy from the sun, moon, and planets of the solar system and is based on astrology. Lunar and solar magick are also examples of planetary magick. Full moon rituals are a mixture of natural and planetary magick. To perform planetary magick, you need a good knowledge of astrology and astronomy. An ample amount of preparation goes into this type of magick.

Chaos Magick

This type of magick draws energy from your psyche. To do these types of spells, the practitioner needs to be in an altered state of consciousness, attained through meditation, dance, or sexual intercourse. Once you have attained this state, you can charge your spell with your energy that has built up, as if you were programming the universe and your subconscious at the same time. Chaos magick does not require a lot of preparation. There are no rules to chaos magick, so you can feel free to be creative and experiment as you feel. But continually keep in thought the rules of magick.

Ceremonial Magick

Ceremonial magick is an ancient form of magick using sets of rules, rituals, symbols, and tools. One can consider it the most occult form of magick. The witch needs to be initiated into it by a member of the Institute of Hermetic Studies, the Society of the Inner Light, Templars, Golden Dawn, or Freemasonry before he or she can practice it. The spells need a lot of knowledge and planning. This type of magick is based on Kabbalah and alchemy.

Summoning Magick

Summoning magick draws its energy from entities such as Gods, Goddesses, Ancestors, Faeries, Spirit Animals, Angels, and Demons. These types of spells and rituals require you to summon an entity. You do not need to be religious for these types of spells to work, but you must believe in the entities that you are working with to summon them. If you want an entity to grant your wishes, you will need to create a relationship with them and take the time to do so. Also, keep in mind that you do not choose your spirit guide or ancestor; they will accept you. This is considered the most potent form of summoning magick. This magick should also be given significant consideration, especially with your intentions for the entity.

White Magick

The term white magick may give you the image of a magician conjuring rabbits out of hats, but it is so much more. A magician who does tricks does not practice magick but illusion instead, and illusion is not magick. Some Wiccans don't like the idea of white magick at all, as it may appear to weaken its power or efficacy. This is not the case though. Magick is magick, and the designation of white magick, good magick and black magick, or bad magick is all based on what you are using your magickal practice for.

When we think of magick from a commercial or consumerist perspective, white magick is usually the form that ordinary people will be familiar with. People like traditional healers, gypsies, and fortune-tellers will sell love potions and magickal bags to bring you fortune and oils to anoint your wallet. This is often not the real thing and is more snake oil than anything else.

One of the tenets of Wicca is that of the principle of threefold. Everything you do will always return to you threefold, and so this encourages Wiccans to solely practice white magick because they are well aware that whatever they send out, they will receive multiplied.

Wicca is primarily considered white magick as it is a holistic, nature-based spiritual practice filled with love and light.

However, while Christianity frowned upon practicing magic, white magick is commonly practiced along with the worship of the deity or deities in many other global religions.

White magick is used for selfless purposes; practitioners who practice white magick are often called healers or white witches. White magick is practiced through healing, blessing, charms, prayers, and songs. White magick pursues the ethics of kindness and goodness. Many traditions of white magick can be traced back to the early worship of local Gods and Goddesses. White magick is also referred to as high magick, and the purpose of this type of magick is to do good or bring a practitioner to a higher state of consciousness. White magick includes gaining divine knowledge, embracing your destiny, attracting luck and love, and driving away evil forces, curing illnesses, finding lost items, controlling the weather, and generating well-being.

Black Magick

When we think of black magick, we can see images of witches with boils on their noses, cackling into a cauldron of bubbling green frog stew. Others may get the idea of Satanists sacrificing cats for power. These are probably far from the truth as black magick is simply magick used to evil ends. The concept of hedonism falls into black magic as well as the practitioner may use their magick for self-serving means such as to procure vast wealth or force someone to fall in love with them.

Black magick is the use of power for evil and selfish purposes. Black magic is also known as low magick and is malicious and used to do harm. Black magick includes invoking demons and evil spirits, hexing and cursing others. This type of magick is also considered bad magick and is used by those who wish to harm others instead of heal or help others.

Black magick is generally considered the use of magick for malevolent, self-serving, and evil ends. Black magick is the polar opposite of white magick in that it is used for evil, while white magick is used for good. Black magick may have gotten more of a bad rap than it deserved as some magickal practitioners such as Alistair Crowley were labeled as a black magician by those who opposed them.

At one point, all magick was thought to be black magick. It was punishable by death, as the British theologian William Perkins wrote in his book, A Discourse of the Damned Art of Witchcraft in 1608, "All witches convicted by the Magistrate should be executed." In his book, he allowed for no exception to this umbrella condemnation. He included "all Diviners, Charmers, Jugglers, all Wizards, commonly called wise men or wise women." Even those who claimed to be "good Witches who do not hurt but good, which do not spoil and destroy, but save and deliver" were sentenced to death for witchcraft.

Today, black magick is usually reserved for "Satanists and devil worshippers" as they attempt to bring great wealth and power upon themselves and death and misfortune upon their foes by using magickal means. Wiccans generally don't differentiate between the two in their individual practice. All Wiccans are aware that irrespective of the intent and outcome, their magickal work will have the same effect on them as it has on the target.

7

BEING MAGICK THROUGH THE WEEK

In many pagan customs, the days of the week play a significant role in effective spell casting. The numerous gods create an energy that is the best type of magickal working. For example, Divination and prophetic dreaming spells are always performed on Monday as it is associated with dreams and astral travel. Of course, not all traditions follow this practice, but you might be shocked at how much it helps. Recording the day of the week each time you complete a spell may cast some light on the link between the type of magic you are performing and the day of the week.

Sunday

Generally, the first day of the week, Sunday takes its name from the Sun, our closet star. It personified as Brighid, Helios, Ra, Apollo, Lugh, and Beli. The Sun rules the ego, the conscious element of the human mind, also known as the real self. It is the day on which this power is most potent.

This is the suitable day of the week to perform spells and rituals involving fathers and other authority figures such as your boss. It is also an excellent day to work on questions regarding leadership, money, exorcism, healing, individuality, hope, fortune, work, promotions, strength, spirituality, swift change, God rituals, prosperity, and power.

Monday

The sacred day of the Moon, Monday, is personified by such goddesses as Selene, Luna, Diana, Thoth, and Artemis. This time of the week is given to the moon, in which it takes its name.

This is an exceptional day to work with moon energy. If a full moon occurs on a Monday, its powers are at their most influential.

Divination and prophetic dreaming are best performed today. It is additionally a great opportunity to perform magic by focusing on mothers, nurturing, pregnancy, healing, empathy, peace, sleep, friendships, psychic awareness, Faerie magic, and Goddess rituals, purification, and fertility woman issues growth. Those hoping to conceive a baby would be smart to strive on a Monday as the enchantment of motherhood is powerful, and pregnancy is in the air.

Tuesday

Tuesday comes from the Germanic God Tiu. Devoted to Mars's strengths, represented as Ares, Tiwaz, Tiw, Tyr, Roman god Mars, Tuesday is linked with war. Like Sunday, it is abundant of male energy, controlled power, strength, and endurance, but focuses on the more fundamental nature of the masculine aspect.

This is a perfect day of the week to work spells and rituals involving endurance, physical courage, vengeance, military honors, surgery, the breaking of harmful spells, productive energy, matrimony, business, beginnings, hunting, politics, contests, protection, victory, and athletics.

Wednesday

Wednesday is devoted to the Teutonic god Woden or Odin. Woden would be considered as being the All-Father god of knowledge, wisdom, enlightenment, and combat. It is a direct adaptation of the Latin term day of Mercury. This is why Mercury controls Wednesday.

This is an exceptional time to work on connections, thought, wisdom, self-expression, and the arts. A perfect day for divination, the conscious mind, business, communication, Wednesday is associated with debt, the arts, transportation, fortune, chance, creativity, travel, prophecy, study, and wisdom.

Wednesday brings the beauty of luck, psychic work satisfaction, enhanced communication, and the direct success that it brings.

Thursday

Ruled by the planet Jupiter, Thursday takes its name from the Norse god Thor. The god of thunder and agricultural work, but in other traditions, Zeus, Jupiter, or Juno.

You will find this great day to work magic regarding prosperity, business, abundance, self-improvement, and success. Most abundance spells are performed with just a green candle.

As a sign of respect on Thursday, try a small prayer to Jupiter before commencing any ritual.

Friday

Friday takes its name from Frigga, the Norse goddess of love and transformation. Like Venus and Aphrodite, Friday is linked with love, making this a perfect time to work spells and rituals concerning love, romance, marriage, intimate matters, passion, potency, and friendship.

Friday has regularly been identified with relaxation as it is at the end of the standard work week.

Saturday

It is given to the Anglo-Saxon god Saetere, the corresponding to the Roman Saturn, as well as the Greek god Cronos. It is also associated with the Trickster-god, Loki, and the Norns, the Norse equal of the Three Fates.

This is an excellent day of the week to work spells and rituals concerning the spirit, communication, meditation, psychic onslaught, or defense.

Of course, you can do any magic on whatever day you please, but as I said, you may find certain spells work better on other days. Just keep track to see if they do.

8

THE MOON AND HER PHASES

The Moon plays a significant part in the superstitions and traditions of cultures around the world. For eons, it serves as both a source of light and a means of measuring time. Like its counterpart, the Sun is associated with many gods and goddesses around the world. In both myth and magic, this spiritual body has always been identified with many critical matters of human existence: passion, desire, masculinity, mystery, the hereafter, death, and renewal. Now, the Moon is still an integral presence in Wicca and alternative forms of contemporary Witchcraft and Paganism. Traditionally, Wiccan covens meet for Full Moon rituals to worship the Goddess on the Esbats, a practice followed by solitaries.

New Moon

When the moon is invisible, also called the Dark of the Moon, it is the most influencing time to cast spells about new beginnings. It is typically a time to take new directions and creating new plans established on the foundation of past events. The impact of the New moon can furthermore increase your dreams and professions, so it is a beneficial time for planting the seeds of achievement. For the duration of the New Moon, you will discover that abundance spells, and employment spells have an increased opportunity of being realized than at other times. The New Moon is likewise generally a suitable time to take a chance the future and spending currency, and those who have undergone difficulties ought to make use of this crucial phase.

Waxing Moon

The phase in the middle of the New Moon and Full Moon is the Waxing Moon. This is a distinctive period for gathering strength, development, and growth. Likewise, it is appropriate to arrange your magickal spells for the best favorable time, with that being the three days before the Moon reaching full. The waxing Moon helps the achievement of any actions, whether of an everyday or spiritual temperament. For pagans/witches, it is a period for pursuits, approval, and a time to improve our magickal powers and our awareness of the other world. The closer we move towards the Full Moon, the higher and more ambitious are our inherent power, which brings a new stage of mindfulness.

Full Moon

The Full Moon is the best opportunity time, mainly when it's drawing near Midnight, the witching hour. Your magickal powers and inner strength will be at their highest. If you want more love in your life, this day is the time to send your wants into the universe. The Full Moon is furthermore the best fitting time to give appreciation and to pay honor to the spirits that protect and guide you. Through this time, our personality's outgoing characteristics begin to appear more extroverted and open towards others. Use this period intelligently and develop your spells into gratifying practices.

Waning Moon

This is the phase when the moon travels from Full to New Moon. Casting spells for doing away with trouble, defeating enemies, removing problems, and producing harm are most effective when the moon is waning. Protection spells for yourself, your loved ones, home, and material possessions are best cast at this time. It is also a time when our bodies are more susceptible to cleansing, so it is an excellent time to cleanse yourself through detoxification. This can be best accomplished by way of healing and herbal remedies. You will find that diet and exercise likewise turn out to be easier in the course of this time, with the results tending to last longer.

9

MAGICKAL COLOR CORRESPONDENCE

Color magick is a part of many magical practices because colors have particular associations. The practice of color correspondences gives an extraordinarily substantial boost to your candle spells. Each color offers a specific frequency of energy. In spellwork, the power of colors is applied to bring about a distinct return in the magick user and bring particular strengths through the basis of sympathetic magick. Remember, if any specific color has specific associations for you individually, then, by all means, move according to your instinct.

Red is the color of intense energy and sexuality. Red is likewise linked with war and power, so if you're about to participate in the conflict, whether physical or emotional, it can be a useful color to have. Imagine the bull that sees red. When practiced positively, it can bring about significant excitement, but if used negatively, it can wreck great devastation and destruction. For love spells, it produces more lust than love. Red is also linked with the root chakra. Because of this, it's connected to our understanding of security, and how we relate to the physical and material worlds.

The color pink is associated with emotional well-being, sensuality, and matters of the heart. Close to the color red, pink represents friendship and love. Dress in pink to attract new friends or when you wish to grow in compassion and self-love.

As a mix of red and yellow, orange arouses ambition and creativity. Use orange when you're performing magickal workings if you feel your muse has been quiet lately. If you are considering some fun and adventure, slip on something orange that gets people's attention. Orange is linked with the sacral chakra, sexuality, and emotion, specifically in our ability to create emotional relationships with other people.

Yellow is identified with Air's element; the powers of the mind arouse the nervous system and intellect. Yellow is an excellent color to use for persuasion and stability. To strengthen communication in a relationship or increases focus and intuition, burn a yellow candle. It's a bright sunny color that extends itself to developing happiness. Because of its relation to the solar plexus chakra, yellow is also linked to self-empowerment.

Most people connect green with the color of money. Green is usually associated with the earth and nature and hence contains healing energy and symbolizes growth in every sense. A green candle typically attracts abundance. Green is also a favorite option for luck drawing spells. In the heart chakra, green is used for spellwork related to compassion, empathy, and spiritual love.

Blue is the color of the subconscious mind, spirituality, and intuition. It helps you call upon the peace and patience of the water element with its gentle but powerful energy. A very pure color, blue, can help awaken and heal the psychic mind. Blue is likewise the color of the throat chakra, which is our core of communication. The calming, cleansing energy is used for spells of healing.

A color of mystery and magic, purple is usually known to be a royal color and brings authority and strength. For divination, astral travel, and strengthening your connection with the unseen realms, uses a purple candle. Purple is linked with the crown chakra. This is the bit of us that is focused on our connection to the Divine, the Universe itself, and our ability to know our place in the grand scheme of things. Remember, red is a powerful energy, and blue is spiritual. Together, they bring about not only spiritual strength but psychic power.

White is the color of new beginnings, cleanliness, purity, and simplicity. Appropriate for Lunar and Goddess workings, use white for workings involving unity and peace, the consecration of magical tools, blessings, and cleansing. As an all-purpose color, white may be substituted for any other color candle when that color is not available.

To represent wealth, prosperity, and happiness, gold is associated with financial gain, business endeavors, and cosmic connections. Due to its close similarity to yellow, it is compared with high mental power and strength. Gold is also useful in matters related to the law, courtrooms, and the justice system.

Silver is associated with the Moon, intuition, reflection, and truth. Because of its lunar associations, silver is tied to women's mysteries, the tides, and pregnancy. For some full moon scrying, or any working that has to do with developing your psychic abilities, dreaming, or astral travel, use a silver candle.

Midway within white and black, gray is the color of stability and neutrality. When you wish to neutralize negative energy, block unwanted energies, or break a spell of bad luck that may be directed at you, a gray candle may be used.

For magical workings related to negativity and banishment, black is an intense, banishing color. Black is associated with transition and rest. It is utilized when interacting with the dead, frequently used by spiritualists. Black is thought to be an evil color associated with evil spirits and death; however, in Wicca, it represents the end of something.

10

SPELLS TO GET YOU STARTED

Witch's Bottle

Items Needed

A Jar with Tight Lid

Sharp Objects (Broken Glass, Rusty Nails, Old Blades, and Screws, Pins, Needles)

Vinegar

Rue

DIRECTIONS

Fill the jar half way with sharp objects, then the remainder of the jar with vinegar with a pinch of rue. Screw the lid on the jar. It has to be buried and concealed outside your front door. Your witch bottle will safeguard your home for years. About twelve inches deep, in a secluded area where it can remain undisturbed. If you reside in a city, a trip to find an isolated site to bury it might be worth it.

Ice Spell

Items Needed

Small Piece of Paper

Black Pen

Small Piece of Black String

Water

Freezer

DIRECTIONS

Write the name of the person on the paper, you want to send away. Tie one knot in the middle of the string, focusing on why this individual is troubling you while you tie it.

Fold the paper up, away from you, with the piece of string inserted in the middle. Add a couple drops of water to the paper. You don't want to destroy the name inside or soak the paper. Only dampen it enough that it will freeze solid. Set the dampened folded paper in the freezer and leave there until the condition has passed.

Simple Protection Spell

Items Needed

1 Handful Salt

1 Teaspoon Garlic Powder

. . .

DIRECTIONS

Combine the salt and garlic. Scatter a little bit at each door entrance and windowsill. If you can get all the openings, that would be perfect. It will help stop and obstruct negative energy.

Hex Breaker Spell

Items Needed

Chamomile

DIRECTIONS

Sprinkle chamomile around the perimeter of your home to break spells against you. For an extra boost, also sprinkle around the perimeter of your property.

Good Luck Spell

Items Needed

Candle to Represent You (any color you like)

Gray Candle

Black Candle

Orange Candle

DIRECTIONS

It's best to perform this spell between the new and full moon. Lighting the candle, this represents you, say:

"This candle is me and me in all things."

Next, light the black candle and say:

"This candle is all the bad luck that has reached my doorstep

Trouble, disappointments and tears are here

This bad luck now leaves me forever."

Light the gray candle and say:

"All that was bad is neutralized.

All my bad luck is dissolved

Light the orange candle and say:

This is the energy coming my way,

To get my life moving and speed up the change."

Directions:

Sit quietly, imagine the negative energies being sucked into the gray candle, and disappears into empty nothingness. Envision the orange candle pulling good energy as well as good luck on the way to you; picture the air moving about with opportunities and prospects.

Taking the typical safety precautions allows the candles burn through completely.

Good Luck Herb Jar

Items Needed

Any combination of herbs related to luck. I've given a sample of a few.

Allspice

Anise

Bamboo

Bayberry

Buckeye

Catnip

Mistletoe

Myrrh

Sandalwood

Nutmeg

DIRECTIONS

Fill a jar with ANY combination of magickal herbs. Seal the jar tightly and keep in your kitchen on a shelf or on a windowsill. Place your hands upon the jar each morning after you wake up and say:

"To the God and Goddess do I pray

Guide me now through another day

Let good fortune come my way

Good luck comes now, here I say."

Gentle shake the jar a few times and kiss it before putting it back.

Good Luck Spell (2)

Items Needed

Four Leaf Clover (if possible)

Coin

Magnet

Clove

A Few Strands of Your Hair

String

DIRECTIONS

Tie all the items with the string onto the magnet creating a talisman. Put the talisman under your bed. Keep it there for 3 days, and then throw away.

Number Three Healing Spell

Items Needed

3 Small Pieces of Paper

3 Pieces of Quartz

Purple Candle

Blue Candle

White Candle

Mint Oil

Myrrh Oil

Sandalwood Oil

DIRECTIONS

Anoint each of the stones and candles with the three oils. Create an equal triangle on your altar with the three candles, placing one stone in front of each candle. On each piece of paper, write the name of the sick individual, and set them in the middle of the triangle.

Ignite each candle and concentrate on the sick individual. Meditate about them being free of their symptoms and healthy. See them healthy in your mind while the candles burn. Recite three times:

"The magick mends and candle burn,

While illness leaves and health return."

Allow the candles to burn for three hours, and then snuff them out. The individual should start to improve shortly. You can add some energy to your spell by performing the ritual for three nights in a row.

Abracadabra Healing Charm

Items Needed

Paper

Pen

This is a very simple spell that I thought I'd include.

Directions

On a small piece of paper, write the word ABRACADABRA. On each line, drop the last letter. Abracadabra will end up being A. It should like this:

ABRACADABRA

To: **ABRACADABR**

To: **ABRACADAB**

To: **ABRACADA**

To: **ABRACAD**

To: **ABRACA**

To: **ABRAC**

To: **ABRA**

To: **ABR**

To: **AB**

To: **A**

Once this completed, roll the paper up and carry it around your neck. The belief is that the illness will vanish just as the word did.

To Aid in Losing Weight

Items Needed

Red Candle

Rose or Clear Quartz

Pen

Paper

DIRECTIONS

Cast your circle and light your candle. Sitting before the candle, focus and center yourself. Write on your paper precisely what your weight goal is. What do you want to attain? Write some encouraging words to yourself. Sketch a picture or explain how you would want to look. Hold the quartz up towards the flame and envision the fire's energy infusing into it. Visualize and focus as distinctly as you can. With your feet together, stand and touch the stone to your forehead. Slowly, begin to move it down your body all the way to your feet, while clearly imagining yourself losing weight. You enjoy exercise, eating healthy food, and being committed to your goal. Touch the charm to any area of your body where you feel are problem areas and really need to lose weight. Visualize the weight melting away. Imagine everything as vividly as possible. When you're ready, speak the following words:

"I wish to lose the weight, I no longer need

This spell I know will help me to succeed

With exercise, and healthy food

I'll be committed in mind and mood

I'll be healthier, this I vow

I'll work to lose weight, starting now."

Close your circle. Put the paper in a safe place and keep the charm with you as much as possible whenever you can. As soon as you feel yourself craving to eat too much, eat unhealthy foods, or make other unhealthy selections, touch the quartz and picture your unhealthy desire vanishing. Sit with it and meditate, focusing on success and strengthen your resolve.

Note: Only use this spell if you are overweight or if losing weight would not make you underweight. The goal is to be healthy.

Quit Smoking Spell

Items Needed

Charcoal Disk

Red Candle

Black Candle

Sage Bundle

Cinnamon

Ginger

Chili Powder

Empty Pack of Cigarettes

Matches

Fireproof Bowl

Light the red candle and recite:

"The color of strength is red

The color of power is red

I have the power to beat this habit,

And I will, day by day, and hour by hour

Now light the black candle and recite:

Black is the color, which sends things away,

And lends me the strength to beat this today."

DIRECTIONS

Combine the chili powder, cinnamon, ginger and together, crushing them until they are powdered. Set the charcoal disc in your bowl, light the charcoal and sprinkle your herb mixture on top of it.

Start tearing the cigarette package into little pieces. While you are tearing the cigarette package, close your eyes and visualize the tar and nicotine leaving your body. Your lungs are going from unpleasant and black to strong and pink.

Put the pieces in the fireproof bowl with the burning charcoal. Strike a match, burning the pieces. Recite:

"Now I burn that which has no control over me

This addiction is gone and I will be free

A new beginning, I will see

Nicotine you have no hold on me."

Light the sage bundle, and smudge the space around you and as well as yourself. Smudge the area over the bowl with the burning cigarette pack in it. Say:

"The strength is within me, there is no doubt

I will be free I will shout."

Place your sage bundle in the bowl and take a moment to meditate. Let the bundle burn out on its own in the bowl.

Bring Passion to Your Door

Items Needed

3 Cups Rain Water

3 Drops Lavender Oil

3 Drops Hot Pepper Sauce

Black Peppercorns

Dried Rosemary

Dried Orris Root Pieces

DIRECTIONS

Use two to three pinches of each herb, mix remaining ingredients in a bowl together while visualizing on drawing passion and love into your life. Sprinkle the mixture with your fingers around your front porch, doorstep and walkway.

Triple Knot Love Spell

Items Needed

24 Inches Red Ribbon

Ylang Ylang Oil

Patchouli Oil

DIRECTIONS

Place a couple drops of both oils into your palms, then rub your palms together. Anoint the entire length of the ribbon with the oils from your palms. Trying to place them out evenly, tie three knots in the ribbon along the length. Recite the first line with the first knot, second line with the second knot, third line with third knot.

"With knot number one, my love shall come.

With knot number two, it will be true.

With knot number three, so mote it be."

Wind the knotted ribbon around the bedpost, doorknob or side lamp of your bedroom. You don't want any extra knots in there so be sure to just loop it.

Love Pouch

Items Needed

4 Pink Candles

Jasmine Flowers

Catnip

Small Pink Bag

Paper

Pen

Cauldron

DIRECTIONS

Set the candles on your altar at the North, East, South, and West with your cauldron in the center. Set the jasmine and catnip inside the cauldron. Write out the characteristics you wish for in a partner as well as in a relationship on the paper. Sign your full name to it, and fold it towards you.

Set the paper in the cauldron, and then light it. Don't worry if the herbs don't burn. As the paper burns, say the following:

"With the power of my words and fire,

Bring me love, a love I desire."

Say again until the paper is completely burned Mix the ashes in along with the herbs, and transfer it into the pink bag. Pull drawstring or tie it shut, and take it with you.

Wish Spell

Items Needed

Green candle

Green or white paper

DIRECTIONS

One the night of the New Moon, write your wish on a clean piece of paper. Light your white candle and turn off the lights. Focus on the success of your wish for several minutes. Continue to think about your wish while you burn the paper in the candle. Repeat the same time until the Full Moon.

Note: This is a wish spell and I have it tailored for money, but you can use it for just about anything using the correct corresponding color of your candle.

A Financial Flame

Items Needed

Gold Candle

Green Candle

Patchouli Incense

Pine Incense

Several Acorns (or Smooth Stones)

Piece of Paper

DIRECTIONS

On the bottom of each candle, carve the rune Fehu (ᚠ). Set them up in candle holders across from each other. Set the patchouli incense up next to the gold candle, and the pine next to the green one. Light everything and get the incense smoldering.

Draw another Fehu on the piece of paper, and put your acorns (or stones) on top.

Let the candles, both burn down until they are completely done, and leave the acorns or stones out on the altar until some extra money comes your way.

Abundance Candle Spell

Items Needed

Green Candle

Candle Holder

Vanilla Oil or Extract

Cinnamon Oil

Large Denomination Coin

Stylus Pen

DIRECTIONS

The power of the flame will assist in drawing new financial prospects to you. Using a stylus pen or anything sharp, carve the word "Wealth" lengthwise sideways on the candle and then anoint "Wealth" with the vanilla oil/extract and cinnamon oil. Place the coin in the bottom of your candle holder, then set the candle on top of the coin. Ignite the candle and allow it to burn completely down.

When the candle is completed, place the now wax-covered coin in a secure location to help bring about money into your life.

Growing Wealth

Items Needed

Thriving Houseplant

A Coin

Dried Patchouli

DIRECTIONS

Any plant will do, but a basil plant works better. Just sprinkle a little bit of the patchouli on the soil, then stick the edge of the coin into the soil in the same place so part of the coin is still sticking up out of the dirt. When new money materializes in your life, spend the coin right away and put a new one in its place.

Money Jar

Items Needed

7 Dimes

Small Jar with Lid (I made an opening in mine)

Bay Leaf

Paper

Pen

DIRECTIONS

Write your need on the paper and drop it into the jar. Take the seven dimes in your dominant hand and place them one by one into the jar. As you drop each, visualize it multiplying into huge amounts and say:

Toward this wish, my money grows

By leaps and by bounds,

I see the money overflows.

Coins that jingle, coins that shine

Come to me now, for you are mine."

Take the bay leaf, write your name on it, and drop into the jar. Seal the jar; place it where only you can see it every day, (where it is not visible to everyone who enters your home). Add a coin or two to the jar each day. Money will flow to you from unexpected sources. After you obtain the money you need, thank the Goddess for what you've received. Remove the paper from the jar and bury the paper outside.

Home Abundance Money Spell

Items Needed

1 New Dollar Bill

1 Green Candle

1 Candle Holder

Powdered Cloves

Directions

Rub the green candle with the powdered cloves. Place the candle in the candle holder and position it on top of the dollar bill.

Three hours after sunset, during the waxing moon on a Thursday, light the candle. Visualize the abundance coming into your for a few minutes. Allow the candle burn until it burns out.

The following day, bury the candle remains; pat the bill with powdered cloves and position it in a safe place in your home.

Dream Spell

Items Needed

Dream Herbs (Ambergris, Peppermint, Yarrow, Mugwort, etc.)

1 large All Night Candle

Purple String

Small Bag (in the corresponding color to the desired psychic dream)

Directions

Begin by making a mixture of herbs and plants that correspond to your desired dream. Place mixed herbs in the bag and charge with the purpose you wish to dream about and place it underneath your pillow. You may want to maintain a dream book/journal to make sure you don't forget the dream and your answer.

Candle Magick for Divination

Items Needed

1 Candle

Begin by casting your protective circle or space. Bringing yourself into a reflective state and visualize your need coming true. As soon as you have a strong image in your mind, light your candle. As your candle burns, the energy emitted is being used to call your desire towards you.

If the candle produces a black smoke after you initially light it, it is getting rid of any negative energy away from your need, assisting in manifesting it quicker.

If the smoke is white, your longing will come true, except there may be some postponement or effort before this happens. If the candle flame is weak, it is working very hard to remove an obstacle to you getting your wants, however it might take time. If the smoke is wafting in your direction, your request is being recognized and will be simply granted.

If the smoke is blows away from you, you will still need to keep at it a lot in order to have your desire come true. If the smoke is blowing to the right, you will have success if you use your mind in order to gain your desire. If the smoke is blowing to the left, you are being cautioned that you are becoming too passionately involved in your desire, which may inhibit it from coming to fulfillment. If you hear a popping noise while the candle is being burnt, at that point the Spirit is at work against a particular resistance on your behalf.

Simple Truth Spell

Items Needed

Lapis Gemstone

White or Purple Candle

DIRECTIONS

To perform the truth spell, you must first center and ground yourself, afterwards cast your circle. Ignite the candle in front of you, and meditate on the flame's light for a few moments. Clear your mind of all thought as best you can. Take the Lapis Lazuli gemstone in your dominant hand. Shut your eyes and see a bright white flame with your mind's eye. See the flame growing larger as it fills the whole circle with light. Make this light as strong as you can, holding this image for a couple of minutes. Finally, send this light into the crystal you are holding. Visualize the lapis stone absorbing all the light inside the circle, as it glows brighter than you can imagine. Repeat the following incantation:

May the truth I seek be revealed to me,

May what is hidden

Be brought to light,

As my will, so mote it be.

Close the circle. The lazuli crystal is now charged to reveal the truth of any situation. Before you go to sleep, place the crystal under your pillow, and setting your intention for the truth to be revealed to you in your dreams or it may come to you in the form of gut feelings during the day. When you are not using the crystal, keep it wrapped in a white cloth.

Find a Lost Item

Items Needed

Paper

Pen

Directions

Write down the item you have lost on a piece of paper. Folding it in half and then half again, hold the paper in your hand. Bring to your mind's eye (middle of forehead) and meditate on the item as long as you feel you need to.

To Find What Is Lost

Items Needed

White candle

Candle holder

Directions

Light the candle, and put it in a holder that is easy to carry. Walk from room to room with it, repeating the following:

By the powers of Moon,

Sun, Earth, Air, Fire and Sea

What once was lost

Now return to me.

Let your eyes wander around until you feel yourself drawn to the spot where your missing item is hiding.

Find a Lost Pet

Items Needed

Green Candle

Blue Candle

White Candle

Bowl

Distilled Water

Directions

Fill bowl with distilled water. Place candles as an equal triangle around the bowl, then light the candles. Look at the water and visualize your pet. Chant this spell:

What has been lost I call to thee

Much more than just good company.

Goddess and God, please lend your ears

Please help me find what I hold dear

As my will, so mote it be.

Chant the spell repeatedly while visualizing your pet, remember him or her perfectly, and imagine them coming home. Feel yourself in the moment as you find them, feel the feelings you feel, all the while chanting and meditating deeply. Do this spell every day for one week, if the pet hasn't return within one week, wait one week and try again.

CONCLUSION

Witches are continually drawn by mystery because witches are seekers. There is a deep part of us that longs for connection. By following Wicca, we feel a stronger connection to the Earth and all she has to offer. We are children of the Earth, and when we practice magick, we know that we are more than just our physical bodies. We are everything and nothing all at once.

Wisdom comes to us, embraced by the circles which we cast. We can work magick, whatever our age, whatever our abilities, whatever our faith. It is an ever-evolving form of practice, but we must know that it can be a dangerous game in this modern age. Before we leap in, we must learn and understand that everything we do has consequences, and we must be prepared to be responsible for the spells we cast.

In today's modern age, we must always keep our mind clear of negative thoughts when we are casting our spells and incantations. Being aware of who we are and what our intentions are when we practice Wicca is vital to make our learning and casting work towards the greater good and not towards harming anyone. Through all of these techniques, we can easily practice Wicca in any safe space we choose. Choose the magick that will work best for you and your intentions.

When witches cast a spell, they don't "hope" it will manifest, they know that through their rituals it "WILL" manifest. The "how" and "when" are left to the God & Goddess to figure it all out.

Most people usually get messed up with this fact. They feel that if their spell doesn't manifest instantly, they throw their hands up and think it didn't work. Sorry people.

The "how" it manifests will depend on many influences you cannot predict. You have to TRUST that it will manifest, and let the universe work out the details.

The "when" it will manifest, will be directly swayed by the "how". It really depends generally, on many factors, but a general rule is to give your spell 28 days (from new moon to new moon, full to full, etc.), or the cycle of three moons.

Back in the day, witches would cast a spell and go on with their lives, knowing that the universe NEVER forgets and the spell will come back, eventually.

That is why casting spells is such a sacred thing, that REAL WICCA witches don't do it as often as you might think.

Your Book of Shadows or grimoire should also be a reflection of who you are; make it your own, and don't be afraid to explore new magick areas as you go along. Each step you take is a step towards enlightenment.

Always remember, "An ye harm none, do what ye will."

ABOUT THE AUTHOR

Monique Joiner Siedlak is a writer, witch, and warrior on a mission to awaken people to their greatest potential through the power of storytelling infused with mysticism, modern paganism, and new age spirituality. At the young age of 12, she began rigorously studying the fascinating philosophy of Wicca. By the time she was 20, she was self-initiated into the craft, and hasn't looked back ever since. To this day, she has authored over 40 books pertaining to the magick and mysteries of life.

To find out more about Monique Joiner Siedlak artistically, spiritually, and personally, feel free to visit her **official website.**

www.mojosiedlak.com

facebook.com/mojosiedlak
x.com/mojosiedlak
instagram.com/mojosiedlak
pinterest.com/mojosiedlak
bookbub.com/authors/monique-joiner-siedlak

MORE BOOKS BY MONIQUE

Candomblé: Dancing for the God

Umbanda

Exploring the Rich and Diverse World

Divination Magic for Beginners

Divination with Runes

Divination with Diloggún

Divination with Osteomancy

Divination with the Tarot

Divination with Stones

The Beginner's Guide to Inner Growth

Astral Projection for Beginners

Meditation for Beginners

Reiki for Beginners

Mastering Your Inner Potential

Creative Visualization

Manifesting With the Law of Attraction

Holistic Healing and Energy

Healing Animals with Reiki

Crystal Healing

Communicating with Your Spirit Guides

Empathic Understanding and Enlightenment

Being an Empath Today

Life on Fire

Healing Your Inner Child

Change Your Life

Raising Your Vibe

The Indie Author's Guides

The Indie Author's Guide to Fast Drafting Your Novel

Get a Handle on Life

Get a Handle on Stress

Time Bound

Get a Handle on Anxiety

Get a Handle on Depression

Get a Handle on Procrastination

The Holistic Yoga and Wellness Series

Yoga for Beginners

Yoga for Stress

Yoga for Back Pain

Yoga for Weight Loss

Yoga for Flexibility

Yoga for Advanced Beginners

Yoga for Fitness

Yoga for Runners

Yoga for Energy

Yoga for Your Sex Life

Yoga to Beat Depression and Anxiety

Yoga for Menstruation

Yoga to Detox Your Body

Yoga to Tone Your Body

The DIY Body Care Series

Creating Your Own Body Butter

Creating Your Own Body Scrub

Creating Your Own Body Spray

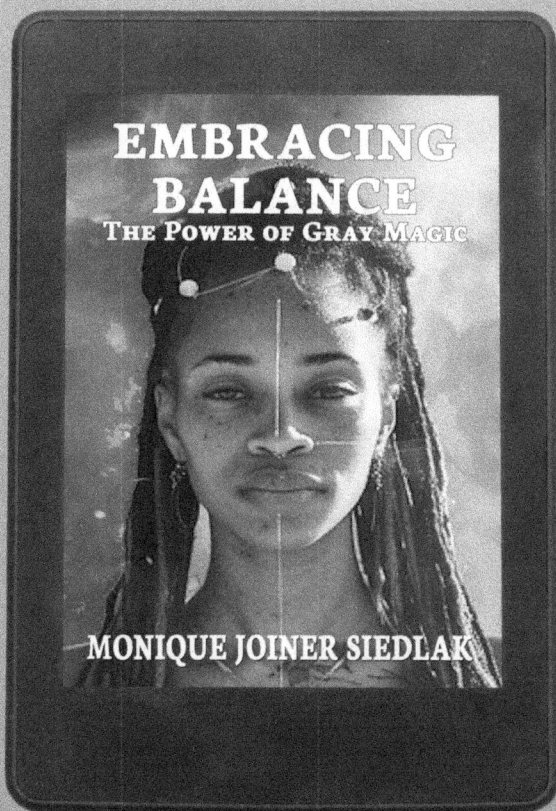

SUPPORT ME BY
LEAVING A REVIEW!

goodreads

amazon

BookBub

Download on
Apple Books

GET IT ON
Google Play

nook
by Barnes & Noble

Rakuten
kobo

www.ingramcontent.com/pod-product-compliance
Lightning Source LLC
Chambersburg PA
CBHW071833020426
42331CB00007B/1711